A Song is Born

A Cantata for Christmas

By Douglas Nolan

Narration by Pamela Martin

Table of Contents:

Performance Time: Approx. 20 minutes

EXCLUSIVELY DISTRIBUTED BY
HAL•LEONARD® CORPORATION
7777 W. BLUEMOUND RD. P.O. BOX 13819 MILWAUKEE, WI 53213

Visit Shawnee Press Online at www.shawneepress.com

FOREWORD

Christmas is a season of praise. It covers our hearts in a blanket of sound and lifts our spirits to new heights. It compels us to tune our hearts and set free our "glorias." It reminds us of the promises of old and the new joy that is ours in Christ.

The true music of Christmas is the music of grace, rich with hope and harmonized with peace. It is the carol of praise shouted by the angels and a canticle of light presented by the dancing stars of night. It is the music of kings and the serenades of shepherds. This glorious song begun long ago still moves our hearts to praise… to bow in adoration before the newborn Savior.

And so we gather with our lullabies of worship at the Bethlehem cradle. We kneel in the shadows in that most unlikely chapel of weathered wood and we discover the amazing truth… that God instead is singing to us.

THE PUBLISHER

A TAPESTRY OF JOYFUL CAROLS

Words by
JOSEPH M. MARTIN (BMI)

Tunes:
SUSSEX CAROL, REGENT SQUARE, WASSAIL SONG *and* **IN DULCI JUBILO**
Arranged by
DOUGLAS NOLAN (BMI)

* Tune: SUSSEX CAROL, Traditional English Carol

11
chil-dren of Light. Draw near and hear your glad song in the night.
11
14
Let mu - sic spread its ju - bi - lant noise.
14
17
f
Let all cre - a - tion find its voice.
f
17
f

2
23
mp
unis.
O come, O come, Em - man - u - el and
mp
sing your song to all Is - ra - el.
mp
Teach all the world your
mu - sic of grace, and tune our hearts to sing your praise.

31
mf
Sing, shout with ju - bi - lant, glo - ri - ous song.
mf
31
mf
34
f
Sing out with hearts and voic - es strong.
f
34
f
37
3
37

* Tune: REGENT SQUARE, Henry T. Smart (1813-1879)

52
soars a song of truth and grace.
52
56
mp cresc. poco a poco
mf
Al - le - lu - ia! Al - le - lu - ia!
mp cresc. poco a poco
mf
56
mp cresc. poco a poco
mf
60
f
Glo - ry be to God on
f
60
f

* Tune: WASSAIL SONG, Traditional English Carol

* Tune: IN DULCI JUBILO, Traditional German Carol
Words: Medieval Latin Carol, tr. John Mason Neale (1818-1866)

87
Chris - tian friends, re - joice with heart and soul and
87
f
90
voice. Give ye heed to what we say;
90
93
95
Je - sus Christ is born to - day. Ox and ass be -
93
95

96
fore Him bow and He is in the man - ger now,
99
Christ is born to - day!
Christ is born to
103
ff
day!

NARRATOR:

The time for singing has come! Let the heavens rejoice! Let the earth be glad! Let the sea resound and the oceans clap their hands! Let the fields be joyous and the mountains burst into song! Then all the trees of the forest will sing for joy! They will sing before the Lord, our King, for He comes. He comes to rule the world in righteousness and His people in truth.

THE KING IS COMING SOON

Words by
JON PAIGE

Music by
JON PAIGE (BMI)
Adapted by
DOUGLAS NOLAN (BMI)

Available separately for 2-part mixed voices – EA5173

10
glo - ry to the sky, for the King is com - ing soon. Ev - 'ry
f
f
10
13
val - ley shout for joy. Let ev - 'ry moun - tain ring. Let the
Let ev - 'ry moun - tain
13
f
15
riv - ers clap their hands in praise. Let the na - tions of the world re -
ring. Clap in praise.
15

18
joice and sing ev - er - last - ing songs of joy, ev - er -
ev - er - last - ing
18
20
last - ing songs of joy, for the King is com - ing soon.
7
joy The ev - er - last - ing King is com - ing soon.
20
mf
23
mf
24
Let the o - cean waves lift a tune - ful hymn of praise, for the
mf
Al - le - lu - ia, for the
23
24

King is com - ing soon. Let the seas re - joice. Ev - 'ry
King is com - ing soon, ver - y soon. Al - le -
riv - er lift its voice, for the King is com - ing
lu - ia, for the King is
soon. Ev - 'ry val - ley shout for joy. Let
com - ing ver - y soon. Ev - 'ry val - ley shout for joy. Let
32

33
ev - 'ry moun - tain ring. Let the riv - ers clap their hands in
ev - 'ry moun - tain ring. Clap in
33
35
praise.___ Let the na - tions of the world re - joice and sing ev - er -
35
38
last - ing songs of joy, ev - er - last - ing songs of joy, for the
ev - er - last - ing joy, the ev - er - last - ing
38

40
8
King is com-ing soon.
King is com-ing soon.
44
45
f with great rejoicing
Let the world as one sing the glo-ry of the Son.
f
Al - le - lu - ia, for the
47
With a joy - ful song let cre-
King is com - ing soon.
Al - le -

a - tion sing a - long, for the King is com - ing soon. Ev - 'ry
lu - ia, for the King is com - ing soon. Ev - 'ry
53
val - ley shout for joy. Let ev - 'ry moun - tain ring. Let the
val - ley shout for joy. Let the
riv - ers clap their hands in praise. Let the na - tions of the world re -
riv - ers clap in praise.

unis.
joice and sing ev - er - last - ing songs of joy, ev - er -
ev - er - last - ing
last - ing songs of joy, for the King is com - ing soon.
joy; ev - er - last - ing King is com - ing soon.
63
ff
rit.
Christ is com - ing soon.

NARRATOR:

In the days of Caesar Augustus, it was decreed that a census be taken of the Roman world. Everyone went to his own town to register and so it was that Joseph, a descendant of David, went to Bethlehem. He made the journey with Mary, who was expecting a child. While they were there, she gave birth to a Son and placed Him in a manger because there was no room for them in the inn.

BABY IN A MANGER

Words by
J. PAUL WILLIAMS (ASCAP)

Music by
DOUGLAS NOLAN (BMI)

Available separately for 2-part mixed voices – EA5180

10
ly - ing in a man - ger, Je - sus, the Lord of all.
man - ger,
10
13
mf
An - gels on that night, robed with heav - en's light,
mf
13
mf
15
sang the news in one ac - cord. Come and see the
15

18
ba - by in a man - ger, Christ, the Lord.
21
10
24
p unis.
Ba - by, ba - by, as the proph - ets
mp contabile
Ba - by, ly - ing in a man - ger, as the proph - ets
mp

27
had fore - told. Ba - by, ba - by,
had fore - told. Ba - by, ly - ing in a man - ger,
27
30
32
mf
soon the world would know. As the an - gels sing,
mf
30
32
mf
33
earth re - ceives her King. Peace and joy are now re -
33

* Tune: ADESTE FIDELES, John Francis Wade (1710-1786)
Words: John Francis Wade (1710-1786)

47
49
Christ the Lord.
Come and see the
50
ba-by in a man-ger, Christ the Lord,
54
rit.
mp
mf
Christ the Lord.

NARRATOR:

On that night in the hills above Bethlehem, as shepherds watched their flocks, an angel appeared. The angel said to them, "I have come to bring you good news, news of joy for the entire world. In Bethlehem, a King has been born, and this is how you will know Him: He is wrapped in cloth and sleeping in a manger." Suddenly, the skies were filled with angels, and the hillsides echoed with the song they sang: "Glory to God in the highest and on earth, peace to everyone of good will." When the angels left them, the shepherds hurried and found Mary and Joseph, and the Baby lying in a manger, just as the angel had said.

ECHO GLORIA

Words by
J. PAUL WILLIAMS (ASCAP)

Music by
JON PAIGE (BMI)
Adapted by
DOUGLAS NOLAN (BMI)

Available separately – EA5149

10
high - est. Peace to all of good will.
13
Glo-ry to God in the high - est.
Hear it ech - o-ing,
16
mp
mf
Hear it ech - o-ing, hear it ech - o-ing still.

19
mp
gradually building
Shep - herds on the hill - side heard the an - gels
19
mp
gradually building
22
sing.
mf
They ran to see a ba - by boy.
22
mf
25
mf
13
They be - held the King.
They be - held the King.
25

28
Glo - ry to God in the high - est. Peace to all of good
will. Glo - ry to God in the high - est.
Hear it ech - o - ing, hear it ech - o - ing
Hear it ech - o - ing,

* Tune: GLORIA, Traditional French Carol
Words: Traditional French Carol

46
glo - ri - a
a. Sing glo - ri - a
46
49
unis.
in ex - cel - sis De -
49
52
mf
o. Glo -
mf
Sing glo - ri - a.
52
mf

55
56
ri - a, glo - ri - a,
Sing glo - ri - a. Sing glo - ri -
58
glo - ri - a
a. Sing glo - ri - a
61
unis.
15
in ex - cel - sis De -

64
o.
Glo-ry to God.
f
Glo - ry to God in the
67
ff
unis.
69
with great rejoicing
high - est,
sing - ing
glo - ry to God in the
70
high - est.
Peace to all of good will.

73
Glo - ry to God in the high - est.
Hear it ech - o - ing,
73
76
mp
mf
Hear it ech - o - ing, hear it ech - o - ing still.
mf
76
mp
mf
dim. poco a poco
79
16
82
mp
Glo - ri -
79
82
mp

83
a.
mp
Glo - ri - a.
83
86
p fading into the distance
Glo - ri - a.
pp
Glo - ri - a.
p fading into the distance
Glo - ri - a.
86
p fading into the distance
pp
89
rit.
pp
Glo - ri - a.
89
rit.
ppp

NARRATOR:

Far from Bethlehem, a group of scholars noticed a brilliant star in the eastern sky. Believing that it signaled the birth of a King, these wise men set out on a journey to follow the star. When it came to rest over the place where the Child was, they were overjoyed. They entered the house, knelt down before the Child in worship, and offered Him gifts they had brought on their journey.

With what shall I come before Him? Will the Lord be satisfied with gifts? Will He be pleased with sacrifices and offerings? How good it is to sing to God; how pleasant and fitting to praise Him! Therefore, I will sing to the Lord all of my life. I will sing praises to Him as long as I live.

to my dear friend, Malone Thompson

I GIVE MY SONG

Words by
JON PAIGE

Music by
JON PAIGE (BMI)
Adapted by
DOUGLAS NOLAN (BMI)

Available separately for S.A.T.B. voices – A6878

9
11
What can I bring?
What can I bring?
What can I give to the
12
What do I have that's wor - thy of Him?
Lord of cre - a - tion?
15
What can I bring to the High Prince of heav - en? What can I bring?

18
rit.
20
a tempo
f
What can I bring? I can sing al - le -
lu - ia, Lord, I a - dore You.
21
24
All my days I can sing Your praise. I can give my song to

27
mp
19
allarg.
You.
mp
27
mp
allarg.
30
a tempo
rejoicing
mf unis.
He fills my mouth with the joy of mu - sic.
mf
Al - le - lu - ia,
30
a tempo
rejoicing
mf
32
He fills my heart with the sounds of His love.
He fills my heart with the sounds of His love.
32

34
He fills my life with the peace of His Spir - it.
34
36
20
rit. cresc.
Now I can sing. Now I can sing.
cresc.
36
rit. cresc.
38
39
a tempo
f
I can sing al - le - lu - ia,
f
38
39
a tempo
f

molto rit.
Lord, I a - dore You. All my days I can
molto rit.
Slower
mp unis.
sing Your praise. I can give my song to You.
Slower
mp
Very slowly
p
I can give my song to You.
p
Very slowly
p

NARRATOR:

Sing for joy to the Lord! Worship Him with gladness. Come before Him with songs of thanksgiving. For God is King of all the earth. With the angels, all the earth bows down and sings His praise.

HARK! THE HERALD ANGELS SING

Words by
CHARLES WESLEY (1707-1788), *alt.*

Tune: **MENDELSSOHN**
by FELIX MENDELSSOHN (1809-1847)
Arranged by
DOUGLAS NOLAN (BMI)

* Part for Congregation is page 56.

10
new - born King;
last - ing Lord;
peace on earth, and mer - cy mild;
late in time, be - hold Him come,
13
God and sin - ners rec - on - ciled."
off - spring of a vir - gin's womb.
15
Joy - ful, all ye
Veiled in flesh the
16
na - tions rise.
God - head see.
Join the tri - umph of the skies.
Hail th'in - car - nate De - i - ty!

19
With an - gel - ic hosts pro - claim, "Christ is born in
Pleased as man with men to dwell, Je - sus our Im -
(us)
19
22
23
f
Beth - le - hem!" Hark! the her - ald an - gels sing.
man - u - el. Hark! the her - ald an - gels sing.
f
22
23
f
25
22
1
2
"Glo - ry to the new - born King."
"Glo - ry to the new - born King."
25
1
2

28
23
32
SOPRANO DESCANT
Hail the Prince of Peace! Hail the Sun of
CONGREGATION may sing melody
S. unis.
A.
Hail the heav'n - born Prince of Peace! Hail the Sun of
B.
32
35
Right - eous - ness! Light, life, all He brings,
Right - eous - ness! Light and life to all He brings,
35

38
40
ris'n with heal - ing in His wings.
Mild He lays His
ris'n with heal - ing in His wings.
Mild He lays His

41
glo - ry by, born that man no more may die;
glo - ry by, born that man no more may die;

44
Born to raise the sons of earth, born to give us
(us all from)
born to raise the sons of earth, born to give us
(us all from)
44
47
48
sec - ond birth. Hark! the her - ald an - gels sing,
sec - ond birth. Hark! the her - ald an - gels sing.
47
48

"Glo - ry to the new - born King! Glo - ry
CHOIR only
"Glo - ry to the new - born King! Glo - ry to the
rit.
ff
to the new - born King!"
new - born King!"

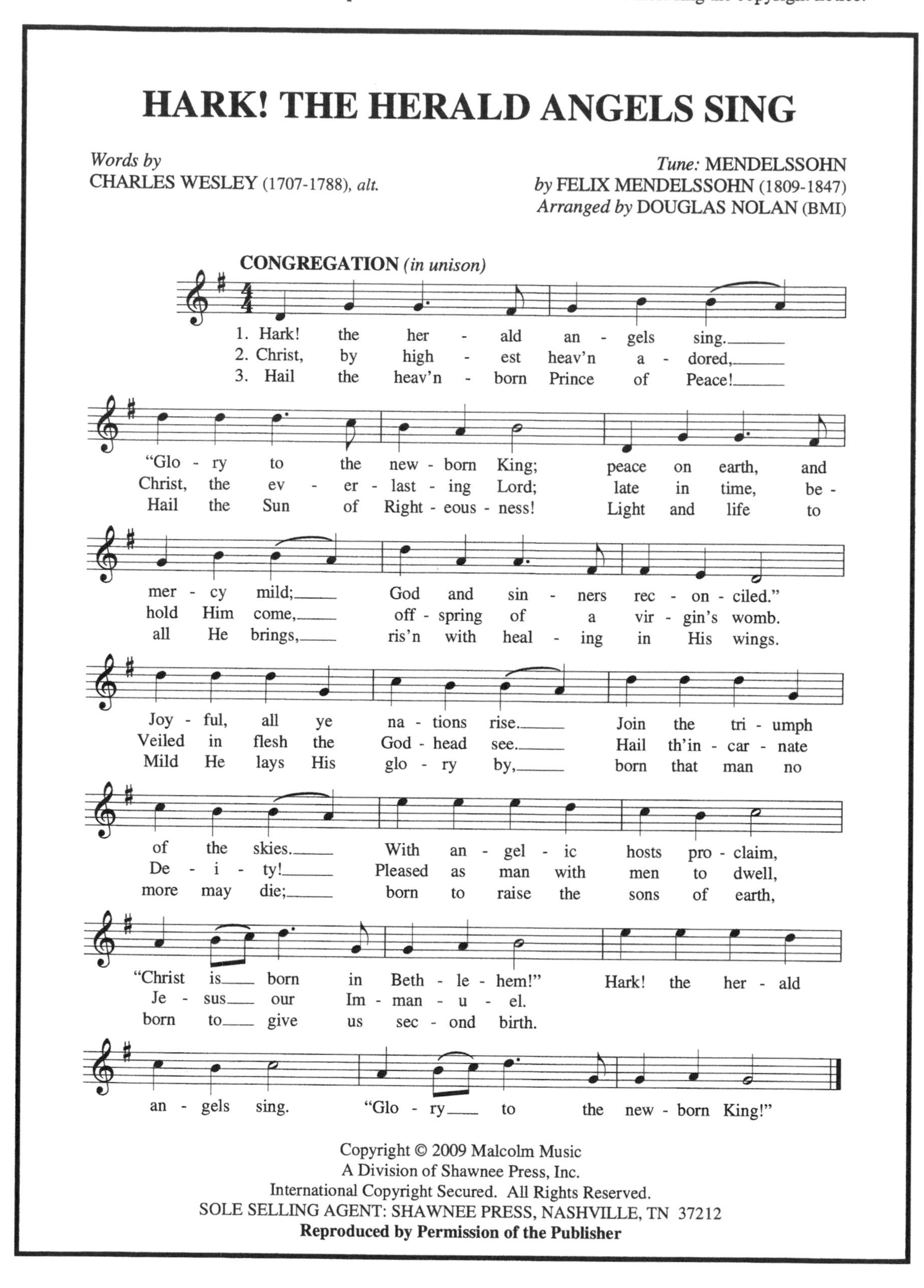
HARK! THE HERALD ANGELS SING
Words by
CHARLES WESLEY (1707-1788), alt.
Tune: MENDELSSOHN
by FELIX MENDELSSOHN (1809-1847)
Arranged by DOUGLAS NOLAN (BMI)
CONGREGATION (in unison)
1. Hark! the her - ald an - gels sing. "Glo - ry to the new - born King; peace on earth, and mer - cy mild; God and sin - ners rec - on - ciled." Joy - ful, all ye na - tions rise. Join the tri - umph of the skies. With an - gel - ic hosts pro - claim, "Christ is born in Beth - le - hem!"
2. Christ, by high - est heav'n a - dored, Christ, the ev - er - last - ing Lord; late in time, be - hold Him come, off - spring of a vir - gin's womb. Veiled in flesh the God - head see. Hail th'in - car - nate De - i - ty! Pleased as man with men to dwell, Je - sus our Im - man - u - el.
3. Hail the heav'n - born Prince of Peace! Hail the Sun of Right - eous - ness! Light and life to all He brings, ris'n with heal - ing in His wings. Mild He lays His glo - ry by, born that man no more may die; born to raise the sons of earth, born to give us sec - ond birth.
Hark! the her - ald an - gels sing. "Glo - ry to the new - born King!"
Copyright © 2009 Malcolm Music
A Division of Shawnee Press, Inc.
International Copyright Secured. All Rights Reserved.
SOLE SELLING AGENT: SHAWNEE PRESS, NASHVILLE, TN 37212
Reproduced by Permission of the Publisher